La Dogaressa & Other Poems

Copyright © January 2018 by Laurie Byro

Cowboy Buddha Publishing, LLC

No part of this book may be reproduced or transmitted in any form or by any means, electronic or mechanical, including photocopy, recording, or any information storage or retrieval system, without permission in writing from the author or his agents, except by a reviewer to be printed in a magazine or newspaper, or electronically transmitted on radio or television.

ISBN 978-0-9994795-0-6

Cover & Book Design by Jessica Dyer

Cover & Interior Photography & Art by Michael Byro

Publishing Logo by Ted Nichols

Cowboy Buddha Publishing, LLC

Benton, Arkansas

Table of Contents

Part One

La Dogaressa Pantoum 1

The Vestal Lady of Venice 2

Cigars 3

A Poem for Trinkets 4

Silver Bed Head 5

Paint and Paint Cans 6

The Beast I Call My Own 7

Bronze Horse of the City 8

Pegeen Guggenheim 10

Ezra 11

Isadora 12

Yoko Ono 13

The Ghost's Confession 14

Jam 15

The Collection at Midnight 16

The Ghost of John Holms Visits Peggy Guggenheim 18

James Joyce's Blackthorn Stick 19

Sparrow 20

Waiting for Peggy 21

Part Two

A Fox as Fey Totem 25

The Ranch 26

Prayer from the White Angora Goat 26

Prayer from the Cow Named Black-Eyed Susan 27

Confession of the Abiquiu Chow 27

Living in the Body of a Scorpion 28

The Rain Child 30

Worry Moths: Lawrence's Consumption 31

Elegy for the Lawrence Tree 32

What Dorothy Brett Thought 33

Exhuming D.H. Lawrence 34

The Ghost Visits Mabel Dodge Luhan 35

The Ghost Visits Frieda Lawrence 36

A Poem for Ashes 37

The Fox 38

What Makes The Fox Chase His Own Tail? 38

The Fox Requiem 39

The Dream Fox 40

The Gamekeeper's Forest 41

The Aging Magician Speaks to His Reflection 42

Poet 43

Inside a Finch 44

A Lyrebird's Tale 45

Snow Bees 46

Send Forth a Raven 47

Lark and Owl 48

Penelope and the Birdman 50

Job Returns as a Puffin 54

Angel and the Reader (1930's) 55

Porch Birds 57

Redwing 58

About the Author 59

Acknowledgments 61

One

"A woman has to live her life or live to repent not having lived it."

D.H. Lawrence

La Dogaressa Pantoum

*"Where I was still told to my face that modern art
can only be loved...by Jews."* – Peggy Guggenheim

Cruel kids throw dead kittens in my garden like rain petals.
I am a Jewess in a town of Catholic ghosts.
My babies do not bark unless there is a reason;
they carry dead kittens like a trophy or a bone.

I am their Jewess in a town of Catholic ghosts.
They taunt me with Dogaressa, think my nose a snout.
They carry dead kittens like a trophy or a bone.
Every night, in Venice, I go to sleep alone.

They taunt me with Dogaressa, think my nose a snout.
I try to ignore them, serve up Warhol soup and crackers.
Every night that it rains I go to sleep alone.
The gardener and I mulch our blossoms with soft striped fur.

I try to ignore them, serve up Warhol soup and crackers.
My babies do not bark unless there is a reason.
The gardener and I mulch our flowers with soft striped fur.
Children throw dead kittens in my garden like rain petals.

The Vestal Lady of Venice

*"But if a girl were possible as I am possible
then marriage would be possible..."* – Gregory Corso

I told her she was old with memories, but the truth was when
the moon sings with dreams and twilight her wedding veil,
I see her completely, as she is, and that is entirely alone.

She collected us like she collects butterflies or dogs, frames
and strange glasses. I think the world is blurred to her;
perhaps she likes it that way. She needs friends, not those

creepy painters. She needs her daughter to wave her wand
and turn her back into a mother. She is a Monarch flitting through
an empty palace. The last time I saw her, during one of those wild

soirées, attended by vampires, she was bathing in the moon light.
From the gondolier she hired to ferry us around, as if we were on
the River Styx, I could pretend for a moment she was young.

We were both the same age. I watched her rise from the fangy mooned
water, as if to leave her mermaid tail behind to join her tortured guests.
They cat-called and waved her back into their amber lit lives.

It were as if she were hiding there among the bottles: a sequin
that had fallen off one of her tiaras or maybe she was a tear.
I looked at the watch she has given so freely from

her own hand and prayed for us both. That there would be time,
Sweet Lady, when we could shrug off our tired human skin,
rattlers that devour the light. Then together, drift off

like one of her Chagall couples into a flame red sky,
a sailor's best omen. Or like that apple that tempts us, leads us
instead into paradise. A place where time is simply a fool's notion.

Cigars

"Guggenheim and his valet were last seen seated in deck chairs in the foyer of the Grand Staircase sipping brandy and smoking cigars." – Wikipedia

I know we have always been mocked as a gentleman's plaything,
but the night we were honorably discharged and turned into ash
like those two should have 30 years later as old-fools, fat and cosseted:

we had some moments of grace. They sparked life; our purpose was to burn out
then die with them. They were in their best Brooks Brothers smoking jackets

debating their few hours left as their Egyptian servant was denied boarding
a first class life-boat. If there be heaven let us wind up in a hero's mouth.
We are of little consequence in a dreamer's world. The dignity of being

needed so earnestly, used and not discarded. After we were born, we became
so important that in early days a man read to us each morning: humble beginnings

saved by literature and learning. We began in factories where only the chosen,
the pardoned can read. Our imaginations ran wild in belief that this story
could have ended differently had they wanted. That a Count is the equal

to a sailor, or a slave. Mercy and hope are more than mere words. Our patrons
chose not to spend their money to purchase their souls. They could have saved

themselves but decided that each woman or child is precious to the earth,
that in the end all human beings are equal and not defined by coin
but by character, that it was their duty as gentlemen to be taken by the sea.

A Poem for Trinkets

"I wore one of my Tanguy earrings and one made by Calder in order to show my impartiality between Surrealist and Abstract Art."
– Peggy Guggenheim

She said she was impartial to us, but I suspect otherwise,
when we were alone, I knew she preferred me to my angular brother.

I am an oval, you see, and until the day she died, her life was a skeletal
subterfuge. Often she disappeared into me, walked among my sepia

columns. I was a safe place for her. She said hello to my cobwebbed
branches, held me like a lover, murmured into my shell-ear. My twin was

a blue iris, I was brown, she longed not to be held prisoner in a Jew hating
world. After she would disappear into me and return back, summoned

by the clink of glasses, fork on dessert plate, to those dreary drunken
parties, I missed her then. Calder? She professed an affinity to his

madness, his unsteady walks. His floors shot out from under him, if you
glanced up you became confused. I say her life was unsteady enough

to want the terra firma of me. There among those savage
artists, she was a lightning rod scepter always releasing herself

to an unreliable sky. Heaven for her was the collecting of odd things,
jolie laide the French say, bijous around a pimpled virgin's neck. Oh

the messiness of beauty. They would call her *jolie laide*: sniff
at her clumsy grace: to me she was a witchy Prospero. I knew

she coveted a round life to a willowy dowser's stick. I was her
scry bowl, a landscape to disappear into, her Eden in a globe.

A fortune in a steady hand, I was the framed magic spell she wore
to bed at night, hopeful that I would promise her a happy ending.

Silver Bed Head

After Alexander Calder

Silver veil of hair, an aged mermaid, waterfall
of fish and plant, make me a headboard

that summons dreams. Fashion a water globe hookah
that percolates over us pumping, pulsing vaporous

thoughts escaping into ecstatic lake weed. When our
footprints dissolve into froth and sand, bubble

into the corners of a witch's brew mouth, then
we will know the truth of it. People love filth.

Bread and sex: my sins are common ones.
Lift my imagination into the wild air,

never shackle me into the harness of a messy
bed. My headboard breathes and silver

fish carry me down stream. Men? I used them all,
sad darlings, in order to perform a scurrilous trance.

We are butterflies in moonlight. Into each drifter's
arms, let us begin the dance.

Paint and Paint Cans

*"I continue to get further away from the usual painter's tools
such as easel, palette, brushes, etc."* – Jackson Pollock

He used us, but he used us to create beauty. Before our life with him we were
fluid: a possibility, something that could only become. When he

released us to the air, popped off our tops like a cork, we shivered in anticipation.
We wanted to wrinkle and dry before him but it was too late for regrets.

He produced gaiety, whisked us bodily around and around: we pirouetted,
rumbaed. We circled him like a coven of angels. We spilled our guts

for him. My friends smeared the floor and his body with us. He jabbed
into us over and over with sticks, with screw drivers with anything

he could find. He was cock sure, he knew how we liked to be touched.
He knew us like the sweat on the forehead of Michelangelo, like the dewy

slop off a St. Bernard's tongue. He seduced us, we seduced him.
We covered him in a wild array of vines, of every blooming flower.

We took him to our tin chests and worshiped him. He emptied us, then
dented and rejected, he lined us all around the room where we stayed

barren and discarded, but close to our other selves. In the end we were
in paradise. We were evolved in a matter of minutes, in a matter of days,

We became attached to our new lives. We entertained each other in
a brave new world. Joyous we held each other tight, and knew that

by squandering us he had somehow saved us. We knew by our deaths
we were never given false hope. We worshiped him as our new God.

The Beast I Call My Own

In memory of Lee Krasner

"I don't paint nature. I am Nature." – Jackson Pollock

Another time, dunes dissolving like tears as we wrap
each other in blankets of regret, Jack sips his iced tea, crushes

ice like he wants to pour it into a flask and me not caring.
He is sober. That is all. Brilliant and sober, even drunk

he bests them, even in bed, de Kooning knows it. He rode
in from Cody, Wyoming, lassoed me and then the world

with his lariats of paint. Even Peggy with her crotchless
panties has an eye for art. Except mine. I am that LK person

she despises, I am used to walking two steps behind.
You would think it would help that we are members

of the same tribe, self-loathing Jewess whore.
Still I trust her more than the others to keep my Beast in line.

Shrinks telling him to drink all he wants, not one understands
a "real" alcoholic. He is a "real" artist, this one, and so am I

if talent counts for anything. If he is Caliban that would make me
Sycorax and what then? Rimbaud would have hated me for translating

that line on my studio wall as "The beast I call my own" and yet
he didn't know Jack did he? For that matter, did anyone?

Laurie Byro

Bronze Horse of the City

After Marini Marino horses

"To describe and explain my ideas is to lose them." – Marini Marino

If she had ridden me, if she had ridden me wild, my lady–
she in butterflies, me, a bronze pet, black hairstreak, winged-child,

a tax weary bride, peasants averting their eyes, perhaps then,
I would have been royal and proud, dignified and lost this mask

of anguish. Imagine me in her garden then, light shining off
my ruddy head, and she all–again I state the obvious, all

in powdery moth: monarchs, chalk hill blue, checkered skippers,
dark green fritillary, what a thrill to be covered as in autumn leaves,

this falling, detached, not beholden to a tree. She, brimstone
gate keeper: softest wings, purest thighs. She would leave her palace

door, I am forever trapped in her garden, stuck,
while deer and rabbits run long side. With a peek of a stream just

beyond the gate, I wait. She releases me, patiently I wait. When I strain
bronze muscles, my metal neck quivering, I glimpse

coppery fish, stars shivering in a silvery sky. Planets and weeds feed
us in a tear-filled marble bowl. These are my kin. This breathing

waif who straddles me proves the world wrong, this is not only her
sin. The river holds our longing. She is a maid who has had her voice taken

in exchange for our strange secret. My metal flesh pulses—tense,
I need to force her to loosen her grip. I am her bronze horse.

Permanently erect and ready, taunted in a dirty man's dream; what
do I care when I live for her? I am loyal to these thoughts.

Four white geese, in exchange for her heart, they lead
us like messengers to the river, necks like poles that stir the cloudy

sky, oars that paddle the wind. Softer than a deer skin pouch tucked
beneath her skirt, I am hers: her legs urge, the muscles of her

calves, her touch. We are fevered flesh to bronzed skin, burnished
she rides me holy. I breathe and she feeds me, she plans our wild

escape. Her laughter urges me on. I am more than
a rich girl's mount, a tempest in her yard, a night in armor.

Pegeen Guggenheim

"I paint flowers so they will not die." – Frida Kahlo

Since I was born in Switzerland, you'd think I could aim
for neutral, not fast nor slow. Given my circumstances,
that is impossible. I am guilty of various things.

Mother hands out love like giving us a rough diamond,
precious only to her. I am tempted like Eve, but I know
better than to settle for bribes. That story ended in hardship.

With freedom comes knowledge and mother is the
freest kite in the sky. I want to like her, but her dogs
are her children. Loyal, obedient, dedicated to her whims.

Have you seen the palace? It is what my paintings are
when they are most behaved: naïve, primitive, logy-pure.
We are her ambrosial children. In her exhibition of 31

women, I was number 18. Notice the lack of commitment?
Visually that number is a mess. Was I the curvy Tanguy
or the spiked Calder? Why could she not settle for one

or the other? Hear the explanation: *Pegeen, your birth date
is 18, darling, can't you see the sense?* Mother always
puts on a show. I am both stilt-straight and circus-round.

If only she could have loved me unconditionally, without
complications. Maybe I could have left the drama
and loved the whole of me, wily viper, innocent Maus.

Note: Pegeen Guggenheim died in Paris on March 1, 1967, after overdosing.

Ezra

*"The real trouble with war is that it gives no one a chance
to kill the right people."* — Ezra Pound

In Italy, after my Brimstone Chats, they kept me in a 6 x 6 foot death cell,
a cage really, because my poems were such dangerous creatures, they
feared they would escape and sneak out into the free world, growling

and hissing from the alleys of Pisa. My tall shadow leaned over them:
they were unable to mind. I urged them forward, they bit the hands

that fed them. I was trailed and I was tribulated. Worse luck,
they denied me books, pens and laces on my shoes, as if my righteous
old man's body would goose-step straight to hell from a cat's cradle

noose. In short, I was fucked. Why did I denounce that Pimp Roosevelt
and his coven of banker-whores? I needed the money, their enemies

paid me well. I became a rasping, buzzing hornet in their capitalistic
arses. But I also did well by my friends. In 1954, Hem who owed me
said, "it is a good year to release poets." I responded, "All of America

is an insane asylum" yet they released me from the bughouse anyway,
dropped the treason nonsense. Like "pithos" all of the worst parts

of me escaped St. Elizabeth's bughouse, like a swarm of arrogant
stingers, I landed back in Rapallo, a plague on Italy's vines. Finally,
they recognized I was not only a lunatic, but a moron and with that

I won many prizes and medals. One of my greatest accomplishments
however was overcoming my stupid suburban prejudice of Anti-Semitism.

Also, I am a champion tennis player. Just ask Peggy Guggenheim
who I nailed on the court time and time again who says, "Ezra is a good player,
but he crows like a rooster whenever he makes a good stroke."

Isadora

"Affectations can be dangerous." — Gertrude Stein

"Isadora called me Guggie Peggleheim." — Peggy Guggenheim

The rain came down like a dance. Trees toss off their silver
needles like a dervish; a woman gets caught
up in the tarantella of her candles. She peers into the Book

of Thoth. She shuffles her men in the same way the cards
appear: knight, serf, jester and hermit. The rain
has lived through its troubles. The rain has gathered its

coupling creatures and ridden them through the storm.
The cards talk among themselves when no one is looking.
She is falling in love with another man. Still he covers

her body with the sweetness of warm rain. The downpour
is a grand fouetté. The Seine and the Grand Canal are swelling
to their ninth month. She faces the card that is placed upside

down on the table, the Nine of Pentacles. The falcon
on the woman's hand indicates the taming of her animal nature.
She is more than a clever bitch, a braying donkey. The cock

will crow at dawn when she is just trembling off to sleep.
The rain is relentless, it floats swirling scarves set loose through
the streets where she has danced barefoot, blood dripping

off her toes. Rain wraps its tendrils of lacy shawls around
her shoulders. She will shrug it off along with the tinkling
of her drowned children's voices in the river.

She will say goodbye to the messy nests of magpies,
the sheen and buzz of bottle necks; gauzy blue-silk
rain that wraps her body fit to bursting through its skin.

Yoko Ono

"I thought it would be nice to marry Virgil (Thomson) to have a musical background, but I never got far with the project."
— Peggy Guggenheim

Yoko is busy making Toshi a pot of tea. He is too thin.
They both are. Half the time her grunts and squeals mimic

his music, much like the cries of a hen turkey.
She'd be better off feeding him, yet I suspect she does,

they feed each other. Who else but Toshi would have croaking
frogs introduce a snippet of swan lake? Bach and church bells

whisper in the wish tree she insists she will make
for me at the palazzo. She writes little poems, they talk

to one another fluttering in the branches where she ties
them. They buzz like bee-filled flowers. She is trusting,

I wish I had known her when she was a child. She still is a child.
She believes in her fantasies. Feeling like a voyeur,

I glance at a wish that has managed to flutter to my feet.
It is a vagrant butterfly. It says, " I could never

give up as long as the sky was there." We are running
late for our next engagement. She is our Sherpa, I ask

if she is ready to leave. "Tea and peace cannot be hurried.
We are almost ready for a change, I will let you know."

Note: Yoko Ono was married to Toshi Ich'iyangi from 1956 to 1962. She was the cicerone for Peggy Guggenheim and John Cage in Japan.

The Ghost's Confession

*"Love was the one thing I needed in order to live. As neither of
us gave the other what he most desired, our union was doomed
to failure."* – Peggy Guggenheim

Even here, and you won't like this, I use your name for favors—
if you think wealth and class aren't important, you are wrong. I did love

you, in my way, because I loved life and you saved mine. You got me
out of Germany, and resurrected all those paintings. You may have been

the finest woman I ever knew. Courageous, you. I hope my confession
is enough. I hope your whispering paintings will finally shut up. Even now

I hear them rattling their tongues when they come to life in the old palace.
My wife? I was besotted with Dorothea. I never visit her though; she knows

what we were to one another. But you? If I could make amends, I would, Peggy,
I was an indifferent husband, an inadequate stepfather. *Ich habe*

nicht Tomaten auf den Augen. I made no pretense, I used you
as I had this magnificent talent that I couldn't squander. But kindly

tell those paintings of yours to stop witnessing. Tell those decaying
bones of us, to stay silent, to close their eyes and finally go to sleep.

Jam

"Stoned me just like Jelly Roll, and it stoned me." — Van Morrison

As a grand finale, it got so that after each fight, he would clear
the table with his hand, rub jam into my hair. I bought the little jars
with their particular perfumes in mind. Apple Butter

didn't clash with my shampoo, the Tabac Blond, I'd begun wearing.
I prayed the children wouldn't see this. Bad enough, guests
witnessed the sweet potatoes dripping off my dress,

the spatter of cranberries at holidays. The taste of cantaloupe
preserves always reminded me of leaving him. Some mornings,
I'd put it on my toast, a reason to celebrate.

Note: Laurence Vail and Peggy Guggenheim (1922 to 1928)

The Collection at Midnight

"Having plenty of time and all the museum's funds at my disposal, I put myself on a regime to buy one picture a day." – Peggy Guggenheim

It usually begins with the Picasso poet droning on in a disjointed but
self-important way, enunciating each betrayal, putting the rest of them
to sleep. Calder's headboard releases its dreams, fish pirouette,
they are captive in seaweed. A ghost tries to stir them into thought.

The night watchman startles himself awake with his belching snore,
goes outside to sneak a smoke. Meanwhile, the Klee and Severini
are a perpetual party favorite. Universally liked by these residents,
they recall echoes on the dance floor, the chandelier neon colors swirl off

each canvas, comforting those who still catch a wisp of her tired
egg salads, her embarrassing Campbell tomato soup appetizers.
Marc Chagall's "Rain" causes the others to shriek away in horror.
They each know their value to the world, more than one is convinced

this wild scene is acting out. It has a reputation for sometimes
behaving badly. Mondrian, ever the bore, causes no such disturbances.
You could suffocate in that white on white cage he seems to delight in.
Still, they all fear Dali with his wicked cape. Worse they have discussed

those Jackson Pollocks with their bad manners. What if they lose control
again, splattering paint, a drink, who knows what? Those creeps
have been known to piss on their picnic or anything else in sight.
The clocks strike 1:00 a.m. Yawning, it's time to settle in.

Everyone straightens their frames knowing the returning guard's routine.
Peggy could never get them under control either. Alive
or dead, she acted like a spoiled tart. They wish they could get a break
from this tedious retirement, be on loan somewhere. Anyplace but here.

These days are dull even with the gawkers. They strain for a glance
for the world outside where everyone can enter or leave them.
They have gotten quite used to a passing summer romance. The ghosts
of those yapping hounds litter the palazzo with the dead moths they liked

to snap. "The Angel of the City" sometimes throws back his head
and laughs at it all. At this crazy hour, a Giacometti woman meanders
along the gardens looking for her arms, her head. She is unable
to raise her hands and caution a vagrant lady slipper moon, *no*.

The Ghost of John Holms Visits Peggy Guggenheim

Nothing prepared me for you, my Love, not the infantry, not
the Military Cross I received, not the hours I spent on horses,
mucking about in the war. The MC was a fluke really. Lucky
for me, Germans are big eaters and grounded in "schedules."

They were grounded all right, after I bashed their brains in,
don't ask how. I caught them breakfasting under a tree,
quaint really. War is war, I got all four. After that, fool
that I was, I was captured. I got the idea of being a writer

in the Mainz POW camp. I carried that revolver, edgy,
always blocked. I was a brilliant writer they said, except,
I never wrote. Even at school, I sent my mum and dad
blank pages, I was impotent to write. Frustrated to live.

And then you, my best Love. Frenetic days traveling
traveling. You said 20 million miles, and 20 countries,
always one for grandiosity. I do know I wore out 8 pairs
of shoes including some Brogues. I shall never forgive

myself for those wretched drunken nights, never
forgive the waste of good whiskey when I hurled
it like all those consonants and vowels I couldn't muster
into your eyes. Now I weep Gilbey's or tears – God knows.

Note: John Ferrar Holms and Peggy Guggenheim (1928 to 1934)

James Joyce's Blackthorn Stick

*On this day, December 26th 1937, James Joyce dines
with Samuel Beckett and Peggy Guggenheim, or rather joins
them drinking his usual Fendant de Sion wine, watching
them eat. A few days later, January 4th, 1938, after again dining
with Joyce, Beckett is stabbed in the Paris streets*

and taken to a hospital, unconscious from the loss of blood.
A distraught Joyce has Beckett moved to a private room at his insistence
and his expense. Peggy Guggenheim sits outside the Paris hospital
wistful for her new lover, as snow falls: forsaken, inopportune,
dissolving as it hits the warm earth. The street is a mist.

Later, the street is a languid canal, a patchwork of blues,
greens and grays. It would be easy to cross if only she could reveal him
to the world. "Oblomov" doesn't like public displays.
Fucking is just fucking after all. On impulse, Peggy buys Joyce
a blackthorn stick to thank him. The rivers of Shannon course
through the cane. As lads, Beckett and Joyce drank the sap of birch,
larch and sycamore. Now they are brothers in their love of Peggy,
their love of the demon rum. The cane receives the weight
of Joyce's body, his holy touch, with the grace of a woodsman's arm.

Joyce takes it with him everywhere; nearly blind, he finds it steadies
him as he walks. The stick destined to be his companion absorbs
Joyce's drunken secrets, the ill spent or sacred hour.
It neither reproaches nor summons. He never denies its strength.
Just as tales of the carpenter fixing a table with its wobbly leg
steadied him as a boy, Joyce is attached to his blackthorn stick,
and leans on it whenever he stumbles home.

Sparrow

"Living is a horizontal fall." – Jean Cocteau

Confession: I preferred the dark mystery
of a man's body. The ox-horn, the bamboo, the phallic burn,

the saddle, the tamp of the mix. The jade of the fix, the heady inhale,
the sweet cloying scent, almost armpit, almost oozing rapture.

But it was a return to the rose that flattened me,
pricked my balls, it was a return to the stone bridge,

the herb garden, the cuckoo forest that finished me.
I never wanted to end. Each night like air, I denied the lavender

and sage, marjoram, saffron. I could resist all the temptation
sans amour dans ma vie, the slap of the dying rose. Wherever

she's disappeared to I shall be that province's bird.
The obvious blur of song that remains after she's gone.

Waiting for Peggy

"What do I know of man's destiny? I could tell you more about radishes." – Samuel Beckett

It is absurd she has kept me waiting. Again. In the park, on a bench,
at least not having midnight thoughts, craggy longings for romance

languages. I smoke a thin cigar. I wait for her again. Last time,
we were holed up in our room for four days. Only four. If I fail

at this, this time I will fail better. I suppose I could use this anxiety
in some way. I value privacy but the soles of my boots repeat

gossip. If only I were better at waiting. In the meantime, I'll entertain
myself and talk to my feet. The squirrels gather round to listen.

Two

"I want to live my life so that my nights are not full of regrets."

D.H. Lawrence

A Fox as Fey Totem

For D.H. Lawrence

Why does the fox that divides the grass tempt me so?
Hasn't the black whip of the snake hardened my heart?

Left behind, I seem to have a knack for abandonment.
A coven of vixen skulks from its den, stealthy and mad

as dreams. They are a brown crust of sleep that fades
into red-ribbon sunrise. These feral children summon

me; my soul is a dark forest. Like any forsaken creature,
I lap up my philosophy of blood. I have no conscience:

I seek out these scarlet whores as I name my unborn children.
And you, Fox about to disappear into mist, a red gash

of autumn still asleep on my chin. You have charmed me into
embracing my savage self. They call me the disciple of Rasputin,

the Godson of Caliban. Is love such a fiendish discipline: my beard,
pelt red, my dog's head throbbing scandal, my heart drenched

in Holy wine? I am beguiled by sly brides. I have been reluctantly corrupted.
Oh, to be surrounded by vixen in the seductive tapestry of trees.

I have not confessed my intent, nor left my warm bed
of dreams to meet them among a sentinel of fir. If you examine

my crooked heart, you shall see I am both beast and master,
gamekeeper and vixen, a rifle and a thieving fox.

The Ranch

After Carmen Bernois de Gasztold

1.
Prayer from the White Angora Goat

Lord, given my circumstance, left behind
to be treated as fluff and not stock,
I am pessimistic.
Give me giddiness of heart, Lord.
Oh to be of use, not a wandering vagrant;

what is freedom when we can only go so far?
We are a shaggy lot with sour dispositions.
Once, we were groomed, our desires fulfilled.
Now we yearn to be white blankets,
shoulder-snowdrifts, a fancy lady's shawl.

Lord, our lives are pointless, a hobbyist's toys.
Round us up, God, and release us to
some useful place. Like devoted missionaries
the world will be tamed by us. Today,
it is a bowl of sky and hollow purpose.

You have turned us into an affectation,
each bereft of hope. Seer of all,
there is no future in being exotic
with no chance of redemption,
stuck as we are in a dull and common life.

2.
Prayer from the Cow Named Black-Eyed Susan

Lord, let me be worthy of this man who comes to me with love.
After a day of work, playing at being healthy in a dark mushroom
forest, he comes to free me of my burden of feeding the hired

help. Each night I hear his cough becoming worse. Oh his sweet
sure voice, he tries to do manly chores but is almost a ghost.
His strange words: "queery cow, mystery of you,

in your changeless cowy desirableness." Lord let me always
give him something back. In the cool of the evening, his hands are all
that matters, his voice the only one that turns me liquid.

3.
Confession of the Abiquiu Chow

"I find people very difficult." – Georgia O'Keeffe

She called me the "Town Boss" as I was her best guard, but behind her back?
I called her a twisted desert crone. I must tell you, that bitch was never

satisfied unless I filled their shoes with blood. A Catholic reference? I had to
survive, wasn't permitted to be religious. Consequently, I strayed

to the church a half mile away. She was no one's God. She thought she owned
everything. How can you tether a splash of blue, a cumulus or a mountain?

Juan Hamilton and she imagined they ruled the world, but humping her
was like straddling an adobe wall. She was dry and brittle as one of her

bones, he attended her in the same way he could make a dull pot
interesting. He treated us with more respect than she did, I imagine we

were just her pets. When she tugged my ears I yelped and she liked that;
she liked to inflict pain which is why she left Juan everything. By then,

her grubby relatives were just silent shadows and spit. A lion never forgets
his duty, but a cactus depletes the soil. In those days, when I was half hers

and half my own back, I would lap at my water dish, joy evaporating as quickly
as the wet on my tongue. This is how my life went. I was married to her

bones, haunted by rabbits I was too old to out run. A blue plate special sky
could not be reined in like a kite while she chased those eccentric flowers.

To avoid death, I confess, she must have become a tumble weed.
No longer Maypole Dog-Queen, a cruel splinter growing in my mouth.

4.
Living in the Body of a Scorpion

*"I grow old I grow old, I shall wear the bottoms of my
trousers rolled."* – T.S. Eliot

Rumor has it that we are powerful, but left to our own
devices, we aren't that much. A Goddess thought she tamed
us, but through naming us, we were released

from our poison. Words are more heady than life or death,
by swerving a path through imagination, that is release.
Compassion, we have no use for it. Is a man any less

dead because of wishing it so? Are we less dangerous
without sinister intent? Hear what I say, it was a woman
who polluted our stinger with remorse. We are what

we are, something you can depend on. That makes us
reliable and comforting, ancient and closer to god
than to the fickle nature of the devil.

It would be foolish to believe that my brothers and I
are earnest in our endeavors for peace. To exist, we rely
on higher blood, both kinds, theirs and ours.

The Rain Child

"Give up bearing children and bear hope and love and devotion to those already born." — D.H. Lawrence

It wasn't even your poem, the air was slick
with mating. When the rain started, like spit,
you began preparing like Noah, two by two,

to become the half of a pair. I gobbled down
your stories. Begin here: Lover, Noah flood
rushing down between her legs. I, the Magpie,

stealing confessions, this time off a creaky ship.
I hunt down a blossom to prove you've landed.
Your life trickled to her feet, me seeking

the shiniest piece of foil, a wrapper not something
swaddling. The shiny beads of rain begin, I wear
it around my neck like a rosary. Forgive me fathers

for I have sinned. I have stolen the best part of you,
I have taken the breath straight out of your lips
and shunned the baby in the barn. I have described

the mewling, breached echoes, the fragments of dream
and clotted cream, the absent plate at the table.
Now, you'll want to spin my mouth shut with

your finest embroidery thread. You disappear into
your life, I walk through le "jardin du sommeil"
the empty bassinets, the cribs and iron playpens creep

silently past. Whitman is rocking a cradle with his pen, but
you and I, endless, Love. Clouds fill with their determined
douche of rain, wring themselves down upon all us sinners.

Worry Moths: Lawrence's Consumption

Yours were not Luna or Black Witch that climbed
a vine to heaven, a flurry of ladder to heave yourself
over, but more evidently yours became your father's

mine, a pit pillaged of purpose. Mind's dull utility,
shadow-moths knit their tubercular lace collar.
The body's breath bleeds itself raw, each season's cough

formed a green line of reason. Dull remembrance,
the past field of sorrow. Apple trees in spring blossom:
ghostly Emperors, a perfect hour will someday fall

from that tree. Pastures of sputum, mud dust becomes
a bloody bowl of teeth, each loss a halo summoning
Imperial Angels. Your body, once the host

on her tongue, now a reluctant landlord
no longer offering a place to leave your sleep.
Even the pillows writhe with Antlers, with Angle Shades.

Elegy for the Lawrence Tree

The tree of *The Flying Heart* is a siren's song, still and unconcerned,
an old friend who guards my poems. I go to it, make my way like

a pilgrimage. I am half-awake while it strains back to Mellors'
forest, the air good for breathing at last. I sit beneath its branches,

writing long letters, hardly daring to cough, heady with the smell
of lichen and loss. I am adrift in a sea of gamekeeper's moss.

Its boughs are filled with whispers, the moon a cracked mirror.
It shines down, a broken plate of promises. As long as this tree

lives, I live. And after I die, and the next one after me,
its pinecones will still burst into songs of praise.

What Dorothy Brett Thought

*"Friendship is as binding as the marriage vow,
as important, as eternal."* — D.H. Lawrence

You've seen him at nightfall, right before
sleep, ghost-lover loitering in a hemlock forest,

flirting among old oaks, moss-spirit of your shared
history. You nod at the one whose eyes were first-frost

blueberries, who used to stroke your hair, compare
your legs to the swiftest roe-deer. In the afterlife

of desperate love, summers he was all over you,
lapping your skin like waves. Men and one woman

who once sat by a sticking ocean window. Now,
you can smell the bay of him in pine resin, in-between

lovers falling from grace, straying one last time in your
drowsy other life, leaving you just before you wake. Once,

you wandered hand in hand with him into a black wave,
your hair briny and loosened, sea salt and spit

upon your lips. He dark-drifts as you swim towards
his fading eyes; forgiven, what else is there?

Exhuming D.H. Lawrence

I was not always a ghost in your garden, a fox
or jack rabbit dancing beneath a Worm Moon.

We were not enemies, you or I, we held hands
once, then you breathed me into a cloud of fireflies,

I followed you while you cupped me in your hands,
tore my wings off, raised me like Lazarus to be

what you wanted. Was I the quivering muzzle of fox
or a shotgun; your hands shook from touching me.

Often, you offered the rabbit a safe rest yet shunned
me. You and those madmen picked through my ribs,

trying to find a heart. The fangy moon never knew
whether to grin or clamp us in her soft grip of teeth.

Under the orders of Frau Gluhwurmchen, was I the guttural
sounds the old moggie made, or the randy throated sparrow?

Was I the contralto murmurings of the river while thirsty
peasants lay on their bellies to drink? I want nothing

more than to run through a forest again, twining flowers
in the fur of demon-fox, of vixen. Meanwhile, they've trapped

me in this jar among sooty fireflies. Abandoned, I am unable
to rise one last time. I've been swallowed and regurgitated

into the bottom of a pint glass, smuggled like tea leaves
in a cloth rucksack. Useless as cinders there is no fire left

in me. I am nothing but a hank of scorched fur
and broken ears, a forgotten forest to run through, to hide in.

The Ghost Visits Mabel Dodge Luhan

(With a line from D.H. Lawrence)

"I wonder what will give out first, his lungs or his wit?" – Leo Stein

The truth? I loved you both. Frieda, too, if you had allowed that.
Actually, I loved the entire Pueblo nation. Why do you think
I gave you Kiowa Ranch and encouraged you to move here?

23 Fifth Avenue was good for what it was, a hobbyist's Salon.
But Taos made me breathe differently. My world broke in two
right then; Tony shattered it with his tomahawk. Lorenzo,

I imagine what they say about us. That I am a spoiled heiress
messing with dirty savages. But I realize you and Frieda know
the sacrifice I made to bring forth this place that lured us,

that made us spellbound. It has snowed and the heady full moon
blazes wolflike, risen like a werewolf over the mountains.
That is what I want you to remember when you visit me. To think,

Lorenzo, I bought this place for a buffalo coat, a few trinkets,
and a small sum of money. My son, John, may call it
The Flying Heart, but my heart, like yours, has finally landed.

The Ghost Visits Frieda Lawrence

"She was always waiting, it seemed to be her forte."
— D.H. Lawrence, Lady Chatterley's Lover

Ghost, I have read your letters and worn them
like a chemise, hidden like a star beneath my dress.
They are fragile as weary daffodils, soft as a roebuck's ears.
I know you are unable to touch me, except
with my own hands, yet you continue to woo me.

Please release me to my Soldier, we had a good life.
I am an ancient. I no longer smell like daffodils.
What use could an old woman be to any "Spirit"
at the edge of that mysterious canyon?
I sacrificed my mother's heart for you, ours beat

in two bodies. We had nothing to gain; we were not
vulgar. You were my gamekeeper, my fox leash,
my genius-forest. Grubby English – they may
as well ground your bones, filthy foes. But now winter
moths cover me in dust. Mornings, we bake you

and eat you like holy bread. I can no longer be seduced
by echoing quills, a foxy Nottingham grin. You used
the usual tricks, hungry hands fingering me, embroidering
your name into my skin, lacing flowers through the pelt
of my animal fur, the forest littered with us, leaves

scattering in the wind like ghostly hearts. I want to take down
my silver hair, imagine it as ribbons of coal, my eyes flashing
wildfire – oh those pyres we lit on the fields in which we lay.
Perhaps, spirit, you wish to witness me in moonlight
and I shall smell of daffodils and wet earth one last time.

A Poem for Ashes

"I never saw a wild thing sorry for itself. A small bird will drop frozen dead from a bough without ever having felt sorry for itself."
— D.H. Lawrence

Enter the poet

Just as I move from lip to urn, to coffee can for ease
in transport, the eternal butt mass produces more of us.

We imitate ghostly snakes, we writhe and grow
like a runaway dream. We are the mist off Capri,

the languid soul as it enters bergamot air, sea-salt
and goats drenching the pores on a rocky hillside.

A sooty diesel train rocks us in our death-crib then
we are spilled at the station. We are gathered

and cupped in an enemy's hands, reviled and praised
all at the same time. One myth has us suffocated in

cement, unable to leave this place, forever bound
to all future dreamers. In truth, we are satisfied to

sleep in a bowl on a poet's mantelpiece, a pinch
and sprinkle swimming in a Martini potion (and sometimes

morning tea), we taste like lapsang oolong. We are a last
spell as we conjure the unforgiven back to our lair.

The Fox

1.
After Lawrence

Since the war started, the fox was a demon. Rippling the dark
grass like a red braid, he wove his way like a barnyard tarantella.

By the end of August, the light had changed, the wood-edge
bled a brownish vein, the girl tasted copper.

The fox, undaunted, stared the girl down. Spellbound,
she lost her confidence to jam the wooden stock against

her shoulder and kill him. She knew he knew her. He tasted
the chicken-flesh behind her knees, his razor-ribbon fangs

could peel her lips like an egg, given the chance.
She wanted that chance. In death, she wanted the chance

to be his entirely, to be honored as the one who gave
him life. The red sun was setting. The long war flicked its tail.

2.
What Makes The Fox Chase His Own Tail?

The fox is a thief who circles a woman's shoulders.
His amber eyes covet the luster of pearls. In silence,
he resides red on white luster. He is

a mermaid's red hair in the rain,
part myth, and he swaggers brown in the sun.
He slides smooth into a camisole of seaweed.

He is a caboose that steals eggs after midnight.
He tries to speak the words of lonely boxcars.
He hears morning when the train whistle startles.

He is a sly poem that borrows a thought. He creeps
towards a poet's dream.
He smells his own musky hole and savors it.

The fox is an hour spent with a muddy paw. He is
the blood before a broken vow. He skulks
fields and is hardy in the landscape of strangers.

He is the first time the sun rises and parts.
He is a sin to all creatures that go about their business.
He tears the night with his keening. He is nobody's

business but his own. His pelt sheds elegance
to mask his smudged conscience. He cannot go
through the night undefined.

3.
The Fox Requiem

The girl went outside where suddenly she knew the fox
was singing. A singing roamed the woods, in the fields

and in the darkness. The fox grew from the earth, red
as a candle flame. When she touched him, he bit her

wrist. The fox whisked his brush across her face.
It seared the girl's mouth and she was stricken.

He continued to sing. She lay trembling, a burnt
out wick, silenced by the fox.

4.
The Dream Fox

In the year 1918, there was not much food to buy.
The youth stole the dark eyes of the fox. The youth
had fallen from the dark eyes of the fox. When

he lifted his clouded blue-eyes, she remembered
the rabbit and wild duck flying high towards the wood,
that he had shot. Again, there was silence.

A cunning little flame came across the youth's face.
A gleam of red fed the fine hairs on his cheeks.
She put away the thought of him. He walked

towards the wood's edge with his gun. The youth
had stolen the dark eyes of the fox. He was
the Master of the girl. He would catch her as you catch

a deer or wood cock when you go out to shoot.
It became like a fate. The girl had fallen from
the dark eyes of the deer.

The Gamekeeper's Forest

Old friends, Mellors loved the forest when
you were young. The grey eyes of the forest shut
its lids, remembering. This time of year, frost lay

mossy and blue in the cracks, mice hid
in the crevices of stone walls. Rheumy eyes

blur the edges loose. We are no longer held captive
to the boundaries of skin. Tight patches
of blackness hover where greenman fires

were lit. I summon trees to recall floaters and moats
as forest dust stirs and settles. Through the bracken

and oaks, the heart of England rests. Dense and bony
branches fill a cemetery of trees. There is no one alive
who remembers the deer and archers, the monks padding

along on asses. Trees in their hooded robes guard birds
who safely flit among them. This forest remembers,

still it remembers. Brushwood soot clings
to the brown hems of trees. A parade of trees,
like ghostly monks, honor their vow of silence.

The Aging Magician Speaks to His Reflection

After Marilyn L. Taylor

Dear scepter moon and top hat, you've fooled me for a time.
I wrote you honest and fearless, not this cumulus face

that yearns to be open, no longer able to conjure a tempest
like Ariel. This island is lonely; my life not quite golden.

I am the fantail ricocheting the bowl, a fangy moon
about to bite my leash in three parts. Old, older, ancient.

I can't do the trick to join the pieces together. I want the lines
in my hands to lead me to a better life. Maybe I'll pull another pelt

from my hat, don my best toupee, make the women loosen
their hips or lose ten pounds. Maybe, I'll pass for sixty again,

mesmerize all with my silver-wolf walking stick. I'm not too old
for dreams. I don't wish to see their grandchild's graduation

pictures. Spare me yet another selfie. My girl, Miranda, stopped
speaking to me more than four decades ago. I want to lasso

the moon with silk scarves, dance under an orb of diamonds,
set my stick to howling. I want to pretend my bones

are growing tall, that I am not shrinking. I want to be invited
to a masquerade ball at the Plaza Hotel, an accountant

with important numbers to balance, not a fool with the usual
tricks up my sleeve. I want to meet a woman in blood-red silk

that she will use to lasso the moon over us. All my perplexed
rabbits will escape into the free world, transforming me.

Not leave me alone in my collapsible hat, except
for those beasts I have named: Longing, Regret.

Poet

There's a name that takes on status after you're dead,
but alive you walk among the trees, muttering

to yourself. How bleak, they missed all that: she believed
that damselflies had a smell, a witch's cauldron rising over

the lake. She told them angel wings rattle in the forest.
Her poems were a failed writer's "mistake." Bleak, freak,

chic, oh well. Oblique, does a poem have a smell?
She could conjure, but never spell. Even her chums

with their cobweb noises. Oy, she heard those voices.
She keeps racking up words but never a pension. She makes

politicians cringe. There is an illness for what she has.
Words summon her to the fairy houses. She follows vowels

home like a crusty trail. She could never write prose
or something dignified. She had no lineage, her mother was

a plumber, and has no MFA. Sssh, you might have guessed,
her best friend, says he's: earnest. They praise her fast

retort, the word they couldn't remember never mind utter.
You must know her poems were her children, a sordid clan,

brats behaving badly. As a last resort, they praised her ability
to respond with this or that quotation. Left-foot right-foot,

through the forest. Aren't you tired, of this brief and meager
hobby? Why couldn't she be a lawyer and make the trains run.

Gnarly bending limbs, a rough line here or there, a strophe bends
low to the ground. Only the sky should covet sound. She praised

real poets, the cardinal's chatter, she'd hurl words hard
and soft: chartreuse, aquamarine, pearl. A smoldering cinder

became a red thrush about to burst into flame. Listen,
hummingbird rests on his halo, his laurelled boa of light.

After she died, they said, "even in silence she is articulate."
Even then, we wish she'd give voice to angels.

Inside a Finch

*"The same June of the same year a stray canary
had fluttered into her house and mine in two widely
separated countries."* — Nabokov

I'm surrounded by yellow in the burst of flight and startle,
I sing my black-tinged warnings: Don't tread on me or my kin.
I'm your father's voice on the porch, corn crackle as the old man
worries for his daughter. I am the burnishing of copper pipes

as he shines up that day's work. "Beautiful" he'd whisper,
as we would take flight around him. He'd carry his tools
to the truck. When my nest mate almost died, rushing the window
for escape, the old man and his daughter carried him to the edge

of the wind, warming his chest. I swear he was gone, but
their breath lifted him back to the forsythia flowers.
What magic these gods possess. For a time, my brother
became a still branch. Me? A leaf, bursting with song.

A Lyrebird's Tale

Well, of course, I was used to men imitating courtship,
but how many years had gone by since you found me,

your beak glittering like the North Star, your strut
destined to win me over: what a strange bird you are.

Today when I found you dead, no longer able to try
and charm me, white bones delicate as the inside

of the shell I held to my ear, I hoped that is what
this new mimicry will be for you. An ocean bird

or a flock of parrots, easy in your mouth, spray
on the tops of your feathers, the endless sky rocking

you to sleep. But I imagine you just can't get real
that way. I wonder if what you imagined me to be

was genuine when you thought of me, as Queen.
How many of us are liars? When I wiped spittle

and shit after Mr. Wilkinson's stroke, how much
of it was for the neighborhood chatterers and not

what I could muster from my heart? How must you
have felt not knowing if my affection for you

was returned? James, the time has passed for me
to say that I am glad that you have honored me

with your music, that I would sing back
to you if it had been allowed.

Snow Bees

Before you died, you became the snow I walked through,
sentinel trees shooing moths and snow bees, same as

the stories I had been raised on, or the string of pearls
I counted like ivory roses. I wished for the end of winter,

even before that first day. Wrens kept hurling themselves
at the windows, bursting into splinters of wing. If this

were an omen, I said it was because the snow queen wanted
pheasant, tricking the birds with reflected clouds. I apologized

to the air, the clothing of the feathers never fades, a speck
in the eye as the moon peels back its light. How many

broken song birds would satisfy the snow queen? How
many walks through the dripping forest before you became

that crusty wind, the crystals that came down in November,
blinding us all from escaping through the canopy of wings?

Send Forth a Raven

Others had gone before me; I didn't give you
the attention you deserved. I tried to lie perfectly
still: in my imagination, I became my imagination.
You are a mountain waiting for me to appear.

I practice dying by sleeping in the bottom of an ark.
While I stayed still – oh so still in my blue flight –
a field filled with black angels where lonely brothers
write. You say I am a dove or a snow storm

making the world below seem more complete.
If you lift my dark tributary of braid, you'll see
my roots are dark. I write notes to you on the dull

back of silver foil. I wanted to bring riches to our nest.
After all this waiting for land and not sky, I bring back
to you an olive branch, a sweet plant growing in my mouth.

Lark and Owl

Evening, you claim feathers
and majestic flight. I seek
mossy darkness
to pour myself under

I stumble along your trellis, look
for an opening through your window
but you've gone to haunt the woods
or another room

The branches make totems
we distinguish
from dreams

Owl, we are never here
at once. Midnight, lighting trails
with eyes

Mine, closed tight

I, the shadows singing
You, the light

Penelope and the Birdman

"And it is this battle of the giants that our nurse-maids try to appease with their lullaby about Heaven." — Freud

I

Afterwards, unsettled, I travel
for days. The moon's bone, thin and curved,
points to a new paradise. I sweep the forest
floor, cast fishing nets into the pines
above our bed of needles.

I fill the forest with favorite things:
marmots and chattering bats. Of course,
I will add turtles and rabbits. We read to each other
by the glow of wolves' eyes, a string
of starfish, varnished fireflies.

The earth hardens beneath our backs.
I lay this bed among lady slippers and ferns.
I make him discard everything but his Argyles, loop
his pocket watch over the twig above. Bedtime,
we thrust and sing. The watch swings
back and forth, dropping minutes.

In the sleep of trees owls devise
a plan to furnish him with wings. Each morning
he sifts piles of dead birds. He doesn't fear death,
but nor do jackdaws, I'm told. Some birds
flirt with suicide, fling themselves at oak or ash:
titmouse, nightjar, bullfinch, crow.

My lover promises when his work is done
he will return to me. I will knit Argyles and wait.
Birds have given up breath for him. Among their feathers
faith now thickens, and I rinse away
their sticky blood.

II

It's easy to see that his purpose is love.
He unstrings the beads of time in the sun.

It's easy to see that his purpose is death.
He sings to an implacable fire.

His mother was a lapwing, his father
part kite, part nightingale. He carries her

cries back to him, as if they were coins
to unspend time, to unpawn summer.

III

Dear Icarus,

I envy you the bite of heaven
as I lie cradled in the earth. I saw
deer today. I glimpsed a falling
star and wanted to show it
to you. I will be faithful. I am a firefly
captured in your hands, and the forest
floor is carpeted with the dead.
The stars hang from cracks in the ceiling.

How can I be so cold in the summer?

Dear Skylark,

I saw a snake today, a brown
striped viper. I found a broken shell, and blue
was the blue of the sky. And periwinkles
were my lover's eyes, and you are free.
And I have had to let you go.
And I have let you go.

Dear Oedipus,

There was a spider
in the lighthouse, a dry web
on my face. And you have gone
to steal your father's eyes,
to put the moon in a wagon, the planets
on the backseat of your old Fuego. She waited
for you in Rapallo, she is waiting
in Dunbarton. We are all
waiting to see you drown.

Memory spirals
up the gallows hill.

Dear Peregrine, don't fall.

IV

At night the earth shriveled and you whispered
stories in my ear. They were not fairy tales.

If I had been truly hungry for you, if jealousy
had been a chain I'd fastened around your neck,

then I'd have coveted every hour you spent without me.
You recounted the story of a bird who started as a boy.

He set off to bring back his masterpiece.
You asked me to accept this. You wanted me to lie

under a juniper tree and wait for your return.
I am sorry you had no Ariel to carry you

home in her arms. I flinch to remember the magic
your father fed you. I was your lover, your mother,

your sister, your whore: the wine you were looking for
was locked in my pantry. I gave you as consolation

two strangers telling stories among gossiping trees,
together forging an epitaph, their happy ending.

V

on the griddle of the sun
our dreams melting like butter
and when you leave me
to sleep my eyelids will flutter.

Job Returns as a Puffin

This is the island of dreams. From here the tempest
will deliver us into the sea of death. Later
we will be washed up on the mainland shore
without eyes, without dreams, with our little orange
feet curling up like the poppies I tore from the earth
to lay on my wife's table. Each bud burst into
a bead of blood that spilled from my master's eyes.
We are all thieves. We are all whores.

If only I could return to the earth and not this sea
of turmoil. My eyes would blaze with his fire
and not be extinguished by his charred fingers.
I would follow him into the dark like I did an insect
that illuminated the night to the days when I was a blossom
needing the sun and he was the garden around me.

Angel and the Reader (1930's)

*"For the life of a creature is in the blood, and I have
given it to you to make atonement for yourselves on the
altar; it is the blood that makes atonement for one's life."*
— Leviticus 17:11

After the rainstorm, I dipped one of my wings
into a puddle, making it blue to match a bird.

I knew then that my love was a bit of a stutter.
The moon offered herself to me like the Lady's

Slipper I found in a fern-wild grove and it fit the arch
of my foot perfectly, cupped my naked toes

like a lover's hand on my breast and lifted me
to the sky like a ballerina with tulle-soft wings.

You sacrifice yourself to me like the goat
you trapped and roasted on a spit. He screamed

as he turned on his wooden cross. Jesus who lived
next door in 5A never forgave us for the stench

of burning hair. He perched on the edge of his chair
reciting parables until I noticed he resembled

the man from Nazareth with horns that somehow
survived the bubbling vat. It was then you wanted me

gone. I made plans to run away but saw prisons
everywhere, in the rungs off the ladderback chair

where he sat reading to us. In the grove of trees
where we would meet to hunt down orchids.

I began to see those trees as a prison to the flowers.
I stole two more as they grew wild and with your cane

as a balance, practiced the art of rising. We memorized
the book of Leviticus until I finally got the hang of those

wings. I watched while the buildings below became
smaller and smaller like speckles on a blue-green egg.

Porch Birds

"Or draw a heart and our initials. I promised when I was older I'd steal away with him to Mexico." – from Salt, 2005

I knew I would need to remember his voice
for a long time. He kept himself like himself the longest

on the porch, an old man used to work and not rest,
unsure of what he was supposed to do with his hands.

He reigned over the quick bright birds greedy for red sugar
water, studied them like a career, get up early dressing

in the dark, try to catch them asleep in their cocoons
of light. His hands would tremble, helpless to explain

how small they were, these noble bursts of fire. *How ready
they are to leave this place and hitchhike to Mexico,* he'd say,

make light travel on the back of some dull bird. Dad, I'd say
you don't believe that? *When you get to be my age,* he'd answer

you can believe almost anything. He'd look into the shadowy yard,
beyond the reach of his tired eyes. *Anything that makes*

*it easier to not miss company when you know it's time
for you to go, to hurry out into sunshine to a different place.*

Redwing

When I flew to you, when I left
my country of marsh and ice, this joy

was inconvenient. I wanted to steal
the turquoise from your eyes,

to always have that sky to lose myself in.
You dwell in a chapel of thieves;

but I am craftier than you. I pilfer
precious things: a jack, a scrap

of tin. I will hide you in my pocket
like the garter snake found sunning

himself with glittering eyes. I want to turn
you to a leafy face, carry you in my beak

across the river. Don't be afraid—
I am lonely, too. When my work is done,

when I scrape a match along the bark
of an ash and ferry you with the amber

in my mouth, I shall devour your fingers.
Your skin is crystal white when I drape

you across my back. You breathe me
into flight and I preen my scarlet wings.

You bury me in the oak
until my heart mends.

About the Author

Laurie Byro has been facilitating "Circle of Voices" poetry discussion in New Jersey libraries for 18 years. She is published widely in University presses in the United States and is included in several anthologies. Laurie has garnered more IBPC awards (InterBoard Poetry Community) than any other poet, stopping at 54. She had three books of poetry published in 2015 and 2016, her fourth The Bloomsberries and Other Curiosities was published in 2017 by Aldrich Press. Laurie received a 2016 New Jersey Poet's Prize for the first poem in the Stein collection and 2017 Prize for the 2nd poem in the Bloomsberries. Laurie is currently Poet in Residence at the West Milford Township Library, where "Circle of Voices" continues to meet.

About the Author photograph by Michael Byro, from a statue at Pacem in Terris, Warwick, NY by Frederick Franck

——— *Acknowledgements* ———

The author would like to thank the judges and editors of venues where the following poems appeared, some in earlier forms:

"A Fox As Fey Totem," "Penelope and the Birdman," "Snow Bees," "Sparrow," "A Poem for Ashes," "The Vestal Lady of Venice," "The Aging Magician" and "Silver Bed Head"
– *Web Del Sol InterBoard Poetry Community*

"A Fox As Fey Totem," "A Poem for Ashes," "Angel and the Reader," "Confessions of the Abiquiu Chow," "Prayer from the Cow Named Black Eyed Susan," "The Collection at Midnight," and "The Ghost Visits Mabel Doge Luhan" – *Synchronized Chaos*

"Elegy For the Lawrence Tree," "Exhuming D.H. Lawrence," "The Ghost Visits Frieda Lawrence," "The Rain Child"
– *Verse Virtual*

"Inside a Finch," and "Porch Birds" – *Loch Raven Review*

"Job Returns as a Puffin" and "Redwing"– *Scarlet Leaf Review*

"Lark and Owl" – *Miller's Pond Poetry Magazine*

"Lyrebird's Tale," "Snow Bees" – *THAT Literary Review*

"Prayer from the White Angora"– *Presence Magazine*

"Send Forth a Raven"
– from *Luna* (Laurie Byro, Aldrich Press, 2015)

"The Beast I Call My Own"
– *Jewish Women Encyclopedia* (Lee Krasner)

"The Fox," "The Dream Fox"
— from *Wonder* (Laurie Byro, Little Lantern Press)

"The Fox Requiem"— *Raleigh Review*

"The Gamekeeper's Forest"— *Galway Review*

"What Dorothy Brett Thought"— *Southern Florida Poetry Review*

"What Makes the Fox Chase Its Own Tail"
— from *Luna* (Laurie Byro, Aldrich Press)

A special thanks to Jessica Dyer for her amazing editing eye, beautiful cover design and friendship.

This book is dedicated to my friends and family who have rooted for me straight through the "finished line."

As ever this book is for Michael, and his beautiful art. He is my knight, my home.

www.ingramcontent.com/pod-product-compliance
Lightning Source LLC
LaVergne TN
LVHW021117080426
835512LV00011B/2558